GOOD MORNING CLASS— I LOVE YOU!

Thoughts and Questions About "Teaching From The Heart"

BY

ESTHER WRIGHT, M.A.

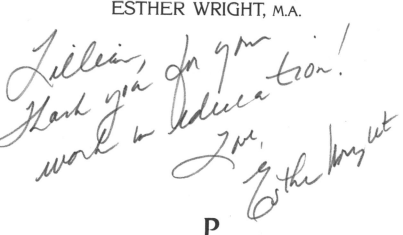

Ɉ

Jalmar Press
Rolling Hills Estates, CA

Summary: Teachers have a unique opportunity to create loving and nurturing learning environments for themselves and their students. Here's how.

ISBN: Trade Paper: 0-915190-58-3

Library of Congress Catalog Card Number: 88-82076

Printing   10 9 8 7 6 5 4 3

This book is dedicated to the thousands of educators who know the agony and ecstasy of teaching young people—and who do it *as if their lives depended on it!*

Bless you for your commitment, your caring and your willingness to confront and learn from the challenges you face as a teacher.

Refresh yourself by reading a little of this book each day and add your own notes to the blank pages so this handy volume becomes your personal guide.

Teaching is the most honorable of professions. It requires extraordinary commitment, vitality and love.

Teachers are called upon to be all knowing, ever caring, willing to sacrifice and able to withstand the ever-constant drama that unfolds in the laboratory of life we call a classroom.

Teaching provides us with joyous moments, tense moments, chaotic moments and those every-once-in-a-while moments when we wonder if we should have gotten a real estate license instead of a teaching credential.

A TEACHER'S CREED

There is no greater gift one human being can give another than the opportunity to learn and grow in a loving and nurturing learning environment.

A COMMON COMMITMENT

Teachers work hard!
Principals work hard!
Parents work hard!
Yet rarely do we fully appreciate one another's commitment to children.

WHAT'S LOVE GOT TO DO WITH IT?

LOVE is a word not commonly used in our classrooms—but it should be!

EVER HAVE ONE OF THESE DAYS?

The kids are all out of their seats having a well-deserved "free period" when the principal makes his once-a-year unannounced visit to your classroom.

Ditto above when the parent of one of your students (who happens to be a board member or a good friend of a board member) drops in to bring Johnny his lunch money.

You get a flat tire on the way to school the day after you have presented a twenty minute lecture to your students about the importance of getting to school on time.

You pass out the final exam only to discover that you are three copies short and the ditto machine isn't working.

The *one* day you didn't prepare a lesson plan, you wake up with a 102 degree fever and the worst flu of your life.

You took a laxative two nights ago that begins to work ten minutes after your class has started.

You've just finished telling Tony's parents how much his behavior has improved when he punches Josh in the mouth and knocks out two of his teeth!

THE STRANGEST THING I'VE EVER HEARD A TEACHER SAY TO A GROUP OF STUDENTS:

"How do you expect to learn anything when you ask so many questions?"

The important thing is not to stop questioning.
Albert Einstein

WHAT DOES YOUR SCHOOL LOOK LIKE?

How would your school look if you considered it "a temple for learning"—a place that reflected honor and excellence? Is a school not a sacred place? Shouldn't it be as clean and impeccable as a church or synagogue?

PERSON TO PERSON

How wonderful it is when we take the time to really get to know our students. . .to learn about their backgrounds and cultures. . .their interests and their dreams. I've noticed how delighted they are when we let them get to know us as well.

Out of this mutual knowing of each other comes the possibility of friendship and understanding that makes for very special student-teacher relationships.

SHARED RESPONSIBILITY FOR LEARNING

There are many teachers who have a real investment in having their students succeed, but none has been more inspiring to me than my son Stephen's ninth grade geography teacher. One evening at the dinner table he described an announcement she had made to the class after returning their mid-term exams. She told the class that there had been two F grades on the test, which she considered *hers* as well as the students' who had received them. She explained that she was unwilling to have failure in her classroom and would do whatever it would take to raise those grades before the final exam (including intensive tutoring before and after school for the students with the failing test scores).

I remember feeling a deep sense of appreciation that this woman was my son's teacher. And I saw that in addition to teaching geography to her students, she was teaching them a thing or two about support, accountability, partnership and responsibility.

CONTROVERSIAL QUESTIONS...

Why is it that most of our school principals and superintendents are men, while most of our school teachers are women?

Why do schools hold PTA meetings in the afternoon when the majority of parents have other children to care for or full-time jobs?

Who would be most upset if we did away with report cards? Who would be most pleased?

Why are school cafeterias allowed to serve a lunch consisting of spaghetti, corn, bread and cookies to children who require a well-rounded, nutritional meal?

Why are high school teachers with a degree in P.E. assigned to teach English and Math classes?

Why isn't *every* teacher trained to teach children with special learning and language needs?

What would the average life span of a teacher be if we didn't have Christmas, Easter and summer vacations?

DO YOU BELIEVE IN MIRACLES?

When *kids* are trusted, respected, loved and supported—MIRACLES HAPPEN!

When *teachers* are trusted, respected, loved and supported—MIRACLES HAPPEN!

When *principals* are trusted, respected, loved and supported—MIRACLES HAPPEN!

MY FAVORITE TEACHER

My father, a product of the Depression, had always wanted to be a teacher. Marrying during the war and fathering three children in his early twenties made college an impossibility. Instead he became a plumber, all the while sharing his thoughts and wisdom with his children (who were not always the attentive listeners he hoped we would be).

Upon retiring a few years ago, he applied to be a school volunteer so that he could work in a classroom. The counselor who interviewed him mentioned that a private vocational high school in the area was desperately seeking a plumbing instructor and that no teaching credential was required. My father applied for the position and was hired on the spot! My dear dad loves his new career! And his students have the good fortune of working with a man who waited a lifetime to accomplish his dream.

HOW ARE WE LISTENING?

When a student is disruptive, he or she is telling us something.

The important thing is whether we are listening with our hearts or our egos.

> *It is only with the heart that one can see rightly. What is essential is invisible to the eye.*
> Antoine de Saint Exupéry

MY DREAM CLASSROOM

All the students come into the classroom on time, well groomed, smiling and eager to begin the new day.

They ask thought-provoking questions and request titles of additional books they can read on the topic we're studying at the moment.

They never have to be reminded to return their signed field trip forms or report cards.

They tell me (frequently) how much they enjoy being in my class and how much they appreciate how hard I work to make learning fun for them.

They fully participate in classroom activities and discussions for the joy of it, rather than for a gold star or good grade on their report card.

They respect and support one another—both in and out of the classroom.

They do all of the above when a substitute is assigned to the class.

TEACHER AS MODEL

Have you ever noticed that the teachers who complain in the lunch room about discipline and tardiness in their classrooms are the very ones who disrupt faculty meetings and frequently show up late to inservice workshops?

Teachers teach more by who they are than by what they say.

Anonymous

AM I THE ONLY ONE?

When I first started teaching I was faced with a frustrating integrity issue...I realized that even though I had received my credential, I was very unsure of myself and knew I had a great deal more to learn about being an effective teacher. Unfortunately, I felt the need to pretend that I had it all figured out, for fear I would lose my job or receive an unsatisfactory evaluation. I never asked for any assistance—even though my fellow teachers and principal would have had a lot of excellent tips for me.

I now realize that teaching is both an art and a science...It is not mastered in one or two years, but is an ongoing learning experience that requires lots of practice.

I wonder how many of us go through our teaching careers never seeking help in our weak areas.

What does it cost us and our students to pretend that we're getting the job done 100% (when in fact there's so much more for us to learn)?

> *Teaching is an art—an art so great and so difficult to master that a man or woman can spend a long life at it, without realizing much more than his limitations and mistakes and his distances from the ideal.*
> William Phelps

TEACHING IS JOYFUL WHEN:

Students want to learn.

Students appreciate how much we care about them.

Administrators support and listen to us.

Parents support and listen to us.

We experience being part of a hard-working team.

We have enough books, supplies and money to do the job we're expected to do.

We have a class size that allows us to know and work with each student in our classroom.

People sometimes say, 'I should like to teach if only pupils cared to learn'. . . but then there would be little need of teaching.

George Herbert Palmer

TEACHING IS AGONIZING WHEN:

Students don't want to learn.

Students don't appreciate how difficult our job is.

Administrators don't support or listen to us.

Parents don't support or appreciate us.

We don't have the books, supplies and funding we need to provide our students with an effective educational program.

We work with kids who are abused, neglected, angry and unloved.

We work with teachers who moan and complain about all of the above instead of taking action to change what can be changed.

A PAINFUL REALIZATION

I have finally come to realize (after much agonizing) that you can't make a student learn something if he or she is not ready or willing to learn.

A QUESTION TO PONDER FROM TIME TO TIME

If you were your administrator, how would you want to be treated by your staff?

ANOTHER QUESTION TO PONDER FROM TIME TO TIME

If you were a student in your classroom, how would you want to be taught and treated?

DROPOUTS

If education ever gets to the place where there are no dropouts (or a very small percentage of them), we can feel secure that we're getting the job done in our schools. People rarely drop out when they experience a sense of purpose, success and growth. Most dropouts I have spoken to have not experienced that school contributed anything to their present or future life.

What will it take for us to realize that the dropout issue is a symptom of an "unwellness" in our schools? It will not require long term studies and extensive funding to eliminate the dropout problem. . . it will only take making sure that our young people experience *success* instead of failure in our schools.

Nobody is bored when he is trying to make something that is beautiful or to discover something that is true.
William Inge

TEACHING—A MIRACULOUS PROCESS

Teachers are amazing people! We are faced with situations that would throw most people into a tailspin! Have you ever imagined what it would be like to place a high-salaried politician, doctor or lawyer in front of a class of 25 first graders? My prediction is that the majority of them would run for the door after the first thirty minutes!

IS IT SPECIAL TO BE SPECIAL? AN IMPORTANT BUT UNCOMFORTABLE INQUIRY

How many children are labeled "slow learners" or "learning disabled" because we didn't have the knowledge, skills or time to address their unique learning needs?

What can be done to address the special learning needs of these students in the regular classroom, so that they don't have to be labeled and separated from their peers in order to receive an education?

Why is it that after placing these students in special education programs with specially trained teachers, small group instruction and special materials, only 5% of them ever return to general education?

What do these students accomplish by being placed in special education?

What do we accomplish by placing them in special education?

PARENTS AS PARTNERS

I met a teacher recently who calls the parents of each of her students two weeks before the school year begins. She talks to them about the special interests of their children as well as their particular concerns. By integrating this information into her planning for the year, she provides parents with the sense that they are partners in the education of their children. The students get the added benefit of having a curriculum custom-tailored to their specific needs and interests.

WHAT WOULD HAPPEN TO EDUCATION IF...

Teachers were required to take paid leaves every seven years?

Principals were evaluated by the students and teachers in their schools?

Teachers were evaluated by students and parents in their classrooms?

Teachers were paid bonuses according to the improvement in achievement test scores between September and June?

Teachers could see themselves teaching on video two or three times a year?

Teachers voted to rid the profession of tenure, so that incompetent teachers could be dismissed without lawsuits, etc.

Dropouts were given the opportunity to speak to teacher trainees in universities about what they needed to be successful in school?

Parents were required to spend ten hours a semester in their child's classroom assisting the teacher?

Special education and bilingual teachers worked hand-in-hand with regular education teachers to serve all students in one classroom, instead of dividing them up by labels?

MACHINES VS. HUMANS

If our primary job was to feed information into our students (similar to entering data into a computer), teaching would be a relatively easy task. But have you noticed how much we are required to interact with the humanity of these youngsters while we are providing them with new skills and concepts? Children come to our classrooms with their past failures and successes, their fears and frustrations and their cultures and values. I am concerned that teacher training and inservice programs pay little attention to affective issues which can greatly impact student learning and behavior.

I recommend that we begin paying more attention to the humanity that resides in every classroom. Not only will we find that we are more effective with our students, but I suspect that we will learn a great deal about ourselves in the process.

While we teach, we learn.

Seneca

DISCIPLINE PROBLEMS—IS THERE A MAGIC CURE?

The students in our classes who are the most disruptive and least motivated are usually the hardest for us to love and teach. The irony is that they need our love, compassion and support more than anyone else. We have all known teachers who seemed to be "miracle workers" with these children...teachers who could turn these "incorrigibles" into pussycats in a relatively short period of time. What is the secret of their success?

I have been inquiring into this question for many years, and after observing a number of these teachers in the classroom, have come up with the following common characteristics:

1. These teachers are confident they can change the student's behavior with loving and nurturing responses, rather than punitive reactions.

2. They feel good about their work as teachers and do not feel invalidated or threatened by the disruptive behaviors.

3. They do not get "triggered" or reactivated by the behaviors, but instead respond with an appropriate and respectful statement or action that does not embarrass or humiliate the disruptive student.

4. The teachers expect the students to behave appropriately—their expectation is expressed in every communication and interaction during the school day.

KIDS GET SCARED

Fear and anxiety are part of life and certainly part of the school experience for many of our students. The issue is not whether it exists or not, but whether we as teachers respond to student fear and insecurity in ways that *fuel* the fear or *diminish* it.

A point well worth remembering is that a "safe" classroom environment is one where it is OK to fail.

A mistake is evidence that somebody has tried to accomplish something.
John E. Babcock

SPEAKING OF FEAR...

Charles Schultz, the noted Peanuts cartoonist, published a cartoon a few years ago suggesting that everyone involved in education is fearful. Charlie Brown confides to Linus that students are afraid of their teachers, teachers are afraid of their principals, principals are afraid of their superintendents and the superintendents are afraid of their Boards of Education. If Charlie is correct in his assertion, we have an interesting problem to address.... Where do we start?

COULD IT BE THIS SIMPLE?

When students feel supported and successful in the classroom, they rarely act out.

When teachers feel supported and successful in their school, they rarely burn out.

THE POWER OF YOUR SPEAKING

Our self-concept is said to be an important determining factor in the decisions we make and the actions we take in our lives. We, as teachers and parents, shape children's self-concept and self-esteem through the way we speak and respond to them.

Listen to how you speak to your students. What are your words and inflection communicating to them about who you think they are? Who you think they are will impact their learning and behavior not only in the classroom but thoughout their lives.

Be conscious, purposeful and loving in your speaking with children.

Do not underestimate the impact you have on their lives.

QUOTES* WORTH REMEMBERING

People must never be humiliated; that is the main thing.
Anton Chekov

Some people will never learn anything, because they understand everything too soon.
Alexander Pope

I have never met a man so ignorant that I couldn't learn something from him.
Galileo Galilei

Too often we give children answers to remember rather than problems to solve.
Roger Lewis

Everything I learn about teaching, I learn from bad students.
John Holt

*Quotes taken from *The Teacher's Quotation Book* by Wanda Lincoln and Murray Suid, Dale Seymour Publications, Palo Alto, CA.

A MESSAGE TO BE TAPED TO YOUR DESK

I CAN ONLY BE GOOD TO MY STUDENTS IF I AM GOOD TO MYSELF—THEREFORE I WILL LOVE, APPRECIATE AND NURTURE MYSELF!

I PROMISE TO SEEK THE SUPPORT OF FRIENDS, FAMILY AND FELLOW TEACHERS WHEN I FIND MYSELF UNABLE TO TAKE THE NECESSARY ACTION TO HAVE MY WORK BE JOYFUL AND SATISFYING.

I WILL REMEMBER THAT MY TEACHING IS A LIFE-ALTERING GIFT TO MY STUDENTS AND THAT THE LESSONS I LEARN ABOUT MYSELF FROM THEM ARE A LIFE-ALTERING GIFT TO ME.

> *Those who have no fire in themselves cannot warm others.*
> Anonymous

ACKNOWLEDGEMENTS

Many thanks to Bil Krehemker, who put his heart and his love into the cover of this book—and my loving gratitude to the teachers who have had the most profound influence in my life—Frank, Werner, Matt and Terry.

And thanks also to Ed Rosenblueth and Grandma Salinas who taught me a lot about unconditional love.

ABOUT THE AUTHOR

ESTHER WRIGHT, M.A. has been an educator for 23 years. During that time she has taught in both elementary and secondary classrooms. She has also served as a teacher trainer at San Francisco State University and a Staff Development Specialist in the San Francisco Unified Schools.

Esther speaks at conferences throughout California on issues related to self-esteem, teacher effectiveness and special education. She is also available to do workshops and presentations to schools upon request.

If you wish to correspond with Esther regarding this book or have her do a presentation to your staff, please write to:

Esther Wright
P.O. Box 146818
San Francisco, CA 94114-6818

or call (415) 821-0447.

ACTUAL SIZE

WEAR IT—SHARE IT

BUTTONS:

1–4 @ $1.50 ea.

5+ @ $1.25 ea.

Add 10% postage (minimum 50 cents)

Price	Quantity	Total
1st Class Postage		
Total		

"GOOD MORNING CLASS–I LOVE YOU"

BOOKS:

$6.95 ea.

Add 10% shipping (minimum $3.00)

Calif. and North Carolina residents, please add sales tax.

Price	Quantity	Total
$6.95		
Shipping		
Total		

Name _____

Address _____

City/State/Zip _____

Enclose payment with order to:

B.L. Winch & Assoc./Jalmar Press   Rolling Hills Estates, CA 90274-4297

45 Hitching Post Drive, Bldg. 2   Phone: (310)547-1240

VISA and Master Charge accepted: Include card # and expiration date. If you are not completely satisfied with your purchase, return the item in good, saleable condition within 10 days for a full refund.

Toll Free Order No. 1 (800) 662-9662 PRICES SUBJECT TO CHANGE WITHOUT NOTICE

DISCOVER materials for positive self-esteem.

CREATE a positive environment in your classroom or home by opening a world of understanding.

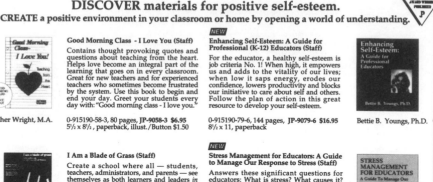

Good Morning Class - I Love You (Staff)

Contains thought provoking quotes and questions about teaching from the heart. Helps love become an integral part of the learning that goes on in every classroom. Great for new teachers and for experienced teachers who sometimes become frustrated by the system. Use this book to begin and end your day. Greet your students every day with: "Good morning class - I love you."

Esther Wright, M.A.

0-915190-58-3, 80 pages, JP-9058-3 $6.95
5½ x 8½, paperback, illust./Button $1.50

NEW

Enhancing Self-Esteem: A Guide for Professional (K-12) Educators (Staff)

For the educator, a healthy self-esteem is job criteria No. 1! When high, it empowers us and adds to the vitality of our lives; when low it saps energy, erodes our confidence, lowers productivity and blocks our initiative to care about self and others. Follow the plan of action in this great resource to develop your self-esteem.

0-915190-79-6, 144 pages, JP-9079-6 $16.95
8½ x 11, paperback

Bettie B. Youngs, Ph.D.

I Am a Blade of Grass (Staff)

Create a school where all — students, teachers, administrators, and parents — see themselves as both learners and leaders in *partnership*. Develop a new compact for learning that focuses on results, that promotes local initiative and that empowers people at all levels of the system. How to in this collaborative curriculum. Great for self-esteem.

Elaine Young, M.A.
with R. Frelow, Ph.D.

0-915190-54-0, 176 pages, JP-9054-0 $14.95
6 x 9, paperback, illustrations

NEW

Stress Management for Educators: A Guide to Manage Our Response to Stress (Staff)

Answers these significant questions for educators: What is stress? What causes it? How do I cope with it? What can be done to manage stress to moderate its negative effects? Can stress be used to advantage? How can educators be stress-proofed to help them remain at peak performance? How do I keep going in spite of it?

0-915190-77-X, 112 pages, JP-9077-X $12.95
8½ x 11, paperback, illus., charts

Bettie B. Youngs, Ph.D.

Peace in 100 Languages: A One-Word Multilingual Dictionary (Staff/Personal)

Accepted by the Guiness Book of Records as simultaneously the largest/smallest dictionary ever published. Envisioned, researched and developed by Soviet peace activists. Ancient, national, local and special languages covered. A portion of purchase price will be donated to joint US/USSR peace project.

Alexander Lapitsky, Ph.D.

0-915190-74-5, 48 pages, JP-9074-5 $14.95
5 x 10, glossy paperback, full color

Feel Better Now (Staff/Personal)

Teaches people to handle stress *as it happens* rapidly and directly. This basic requirement for emotional survival and physical health can be learned with the methods in this book. Find your own recipe for relief by *letting go* with Relaxers, Distractors and Releasers. Foreword: Ken Keyes, Jr. "A mine of practical help" — says Rev. Robert Schuller.

0-915190-66-4, 180 pages, JP-9066-4 $9.95
6 x 9, paperback, appendix, biblio.

Chris Schriner, Rel.D.

Learning to Live, Learning to Love (Staff/Personal)

Important things are often quite simple. But simple things are not necessarily easy. If you are finding that learning to live and learning to love are at times difficult, you are in good company. People everywhere are finding it a tough challenge. This simple book will help. "Shows how to separate 'treasure' from 'trash' in our lives.

Joanne Haynes-Klassen

0-915190-38-9, 160 pages, JP-9038-9 $7.95
6 x 9, paperback, illustrations

Present Yourself: Great Presentation Skills (Staff/Personal)

Use *mind mapping* to become a presenter who is a dynamic part of the message. Learn about transforming fear, knowing your audience, setting the stage, making them remember and much more. Essential reading for anyone interested in communication. This book will become the standard work in this field. Easy to understand and use.

0-915190-51-6, 128 pages, JP-9051-6 $9.95
6 x 9, paperback, illus., mind maps

Michael J. Gelb, M.A.

The Two Minute Lover (Staff/Personal)

With wit, wisdom and compassion, "The Two-Minute Lovers" and their proteges guide you through the steps of building and maintaining an effective relationship in a fast-paced world. They offer encouragement, inspiration and practical techniques for living happily in a relationship, even when outside pressures are enormous. Done like the "One Minute Manager".

Asa Sparks, Ph.D.

0-915190-38-9, 160 pages, JP-9038-9 $9.95
6 x 9, paperback, illustrations

Reading, Writing and Rage (Staff)

An autopsy of one profound school failure, disclosing the complex processes behind it and the secret rage that grew out of it. Developed from educational therapist's viewpoint. A must reading for anyone working with the learning disabled, functional illiterates or juvenile delinquents. Reads like fiction. Foreword by Bruce Jenner.

0-915190-42-7, 240 pages, JP-9042-7 $16.95
5½ x 8½, paperback, biblio., resources

D. Ungerleider, M.A.

ORDER FROM: Jalmar Press, 45 Hitching Post Drive, Bldg. 2, Rolling Hills Estates, CA 90274-5169
CALL TOLL FREE — 800/662-9662. IN CALIF. CALL COLLECT — 213/547-1240. FAX — 213/547-1644